Of previous work by the author:

John Dofflemyer's poetry rings with the truth of the western experience. His language is precise and powerful, his images are stark and candid. As a result, this verse transcends region and touches the human heart.

- Gerald Haslam

I usually avoid reading poetry because I have read so much, and often I am disappointed. But the minute I started reading [this] I sat right up and came totally awake both for subject and for language and style. That's good stuff: I like the esoteric vocabulary too – "beaver lid" and the sweet confluence of cows with motherhood – a diverse set of poems really, political, personal, historical, in the moment. Reminding me again it's not that there need be a "cowboy" poetry but, as we move toward it, a poetry of work and daily life and the land. Which includes history and family.

- Gary Snyder

…exceptional in the force of its vision and the contrast of the humility of its expression, it often gives the promise of what men, women, and life can be; what nature offers for that quest; and always, his words show how poetry can illuminate the way.

- Margo Metegrano, cowboypoetry.com

Proclaiming Space

John Dofflemyer

Versions of these poems have previously appeared in
Dry Crik Journal — Perspectives from the Ranch, a weblog,
and some from the previously published chapbooks,
"2009—Dry Crik Journal", "Uneven Green", and "Elegies",
a limited edition tribute to my mother.

Cover design: Sylvia Ross
Back cover photo: Robbin Dofflemyer

ISBN: 978-1883081072

Dry Crik Press
P.O.Box 44320
Lemon Cove, CA 93244

for Robbin

Poems

Proclaiming Space

*One day a heron walked
up our front steps and looked
into the front-door window.
Was it a heron and also
something else?*
- Jim Harrison ("Suite of Unreason")

PROCLAIMING SPACE

Old white feed tank claimed by two
renegade racing pigeons on their way home
to stay and fill our sky with dozens, colored

wings glinting in unison, once the heron's
roost, our frozen totem facing north, up-canyon
at the head of the drive — our stoic gray sentry,

early on. Or the dependable silhouettes
of a pair of ravens, come evenings to listen
and lean like lovers, closer together until

they disappear at the water trough. Roadrunners
seem everywhere at once sprinting low on long legs
from barn to cactus, strolling the garden rows

like superintendents in tux and tails, also walk
the rail to peer in the window, or the mirror. One
never knows when curiosity might bring them

closer for inspection, for who does the choosing,
who studies whom? And what wide forces
have drawn us closer to proclaim our space?

> *- for Laurie, Matthew and so many others*
> *of the Kaweah River watershed.*

PHYSICS

So much depends
on soil—

tire, wheel and
rain,

the position
of stars

and that distance
of time

between gravity
and grace.

JUST IN CASE

Fog along the creek —
sycamore silhouettes,
limbs without leaves
dance at daylight as if
guarding the threshold
of a medieval forest,
beginning unknown.

Woven with a fallen
branch and seasons
of the ungrazed, a
hay rake rests
among the trees,
not awakened
in my lifetime.

Perhaps Len Bequette
cussed it
when he unhitched it
the last time
the creek ran enough
to irrigate hay,
when the day came

it didn't pay —
or on the edge of open
saved for hard and hungry
times, 'just in case'
like old farmers do —
rusty monuments,
little clues.

STREAMS OF THOUGHT

> *I didn't know that most people*
> *didn't think visually.*
> — Temple Grandin

O' sweet the dreams like clear water
tumbled over fractured rock, mossed
and smoothed, worn through pines

and oaks to spread and disappear
before the dawn, before the day
demands we pray for more.

One must see these streams
of thought, go there, and listen, watch
them pool and find ways through

the timbered granite to meander
open meadows, deer and horses
grazing—walk along tall grassy

banks as dark green shapes of trout
feed and dart upstream, awake within
where dreams and rivers both begin.

FOR POETRY OR LIFE

I will usually choose the worn and threadbare
fumbling in the dark to dress, a favorite shirt
wearing yesterday's fence repair and branding

blood, due respect for its endurance, as if
it had a soul, the comfort ours given purpose
beyond good looks that the old cows recognize

at a distance — a ceremony, almost like a prayer
before I face the anticipated angle of the sun,
season after season. No one cares, out here —

no one judges prosperity or intelligence
by what we wear. For poetry or life in one place,
just the proper fit of word and deed.

TODAY

Unlike any other, the day waits
under dark covers and doesn't care
if you are there or not

to see her details, to watch her
dress — always changing
into something new.

AUTUMN HYMN

Let me wake in the night
and hear it raining
and go back to sleep.
  - Wendell Berry ("Prayers and
      Sayings of the Mad Farmer")

Upon the roof and off the eave:
cascades to soothe a dream
when no urgency awaits,

when earthly strategies step aside
and praise what man cannot create —
let me sleep so soundly!

Let me trust the land endures
man's ambitions, to claim
a holiday for its creatures,

as earth and sky make love
a priority of life. O' musty
scent of after-rain, let me

wake to freely sail among
white cumulus in the grand
regatta of blue sky seas.

WHERE DO POEMS GO?

It was one long poem unfurling
like a river in half-sleep, wrapping
the planet in a ribbon of voices—

old and new, foreign and domestic
accents, a rolling glint of silver
peaked upon each aquamarine

wave like the beat of a song
flowing above the clouds, sounding
the last groans of unknown soldiers

calling home, impatient lovers
and the outcasts cursed to howling
mixed in peace with the sublime.

When it rains, when windows streak
tears of grief and joy, we are relieved
to be human, to be vulnerable again.

MY CHRISTMAS PLAY

He chooses a slim volume of Sapphic verse
from the nightstand, imagines skinny girls
on a Greek isle in the middle of the Mojave…
  - Red Shuttleworth
     ("Gabby Hayes (1951)")

Whir of feathers from the brush, moments
can escape like quail in all directions —
the heart leaps backwards, freezes

as they buzz off to fractured rocks, or
we can read long-limbed verse, watch
sycamores shed enflamed leaves,

first hard rain after the first hard frost,
near the solstice, to dance naked
in the mist of morning, most years.

Beyond the bright lights, a man can
go a little crazy, make do and make sense
of things he thinks he sees, believing.

Somewhere in our brains are big
empty socks that hang from a mantle
with impossible names yet to be filled.

IN OUR HANDS

Knowledge will cure them. But
not all at once. It will take time.
- William Stafford ("Waiting In Line")

The cows have watched, seen me stumble
feeding hay, blade clenched in my teeth,
held their breath each time I climbed

the moving flat bed, wondering. And yes,
in town we step aside for one another,
open doors, lock eyes and nod for all

we have survived and seen, wondering.
We work the shallows near the bank
and stay from the faceless current, trying

to find an eddy in the coming rush of youth,
before another dam is built, or river loosed
to flood. It will take time to accumulate

credentials, or to have the luck to get lost
in the sun's goodbye, or slow approach
to the day—and to save enough experience

to endure our last rainy day. No shortcuts,
it will take time to get to where we began,
to fill-in the blanks, take pride in our hands.

OLD WORDS

There are places to save
things, spots out of the way
of traffic, dusty cubby holes

for lost loves and high
school victories, close
calls and sweet innocence

> banked like candy,
> forever preserved
> to stay the same.

One day, we clean house
to find all the old words
are now meaningless,

so hackneyed and trite
we can't employ them
like we used to — so

we throw them away,
leave them in the Good
Will box and hope

they'll mean something
to someone, fine
words that don't fit

what we have seen —
or what we feel
when they are gone.

FAMILY FARMING IN THE FIFTIES

Mud on his boots, he left
dark remembrances, tiny clods
across her worn, oriental rug

to a pile beneath the chair,
discussing business, bib
overalls agape to flesh,

feet begging to get back
in the field. *I see Louie's
been here*, she'd say arriving

from a pot of soup put on to boil.
A child underfoot, I'd look up
questioning and follow her eyes —

yet never wondered why
he did not stay for the noon meal.
The old house creaked all night,

leaking bits of conversations,
a scattered trail of syllables
that begin to sound familiar.

Some men should be left alone
to nurture dirt and feed us
for neither pay nor charge.

IT'S COWS WE'RE AFTER

"Now Ed: listen here: I haven't an ounce of poetry
in all my body. It's cows we're after."
        - Robinson Jeffers ("The Wind-Struck
        Music")

A bone or two to pluck like harp strings
beneath the petals of tiger-lily skies at sunrise
over sharp ridgelines, men still ride in awe—
words float and poetry rolls off their tongues.

And they dare not whine, dare not succumb
to freezing rain, or none at all, until the work
is done—calving after calving, brandings,
yearlings gathered on the hoof to ship

in circles 'round the sun to somewhere,
out there. 'It's cows we're after' savored:
moments stolen with herds in rhythm:
a cow, horse and the hearts of horsemen

pause that acknowledges the wild gods—
all pleased to have arrived in harmony
beyond the corrals and loading chutes
waiting at the end of roads in these hills.

THREE RIVERS NUT FEED

> *Age brings hard burdens,*
> *But at worst cools hot blood and sets men free*
> *From the sexual compulsions that madden youth.*
> - Robinson Jeffers ("Oysters")

In those days, it was important to be included —
all the Kaweah's loud cowboy sons of pioneers
shaking hardened hands, raising glasses before plastic
deadened the rattle of ice and whiskey, before
two divorces and twenty years of my crazed youth —
one more young one pacing the barbed wire.

Homer's summer nut feed after the calves were marked,
he on the third or fourth of eight wives wed, gold
teeth winking, right-up to his last breath bragging
how he horned the young bulls off — our legend
and proof of the power of oysters to intensify,
to get high and go clear blind on testosterone.

It doesn't matter now that he is gone, damn-near all
of them grazing other dimensions to yet hear the hollers
up and down this old watershed without the biscuits,
without the gravy, without the frittered golden brown
warm and melting on the tongue. Pass the salt and pepper.
A pagan feast of cowmen come to beat their drums.

for Forrest Homer

GREASY CORRALS

After awhile the hills wrap
around you, hold life secure:
the rock, hawk and oak tree

still, sharp ridges holding
our eyes. At these corrals
we are both small and safe,

always. It takes years
to be taught, to wonder
and recognize good fortune

with the fade of old faces
and all the good horses
that have danced here.

for Earl

OLD MEN

So much needs not to be said.
Old men grin with their eyes,
save breath with a look

of understanding, yet
the preachers, teachers and poets
go on and on, searching

for resonance, for the magic
words to open doors, when
all we need to do is look.

LOOKING FOR WORK

In December's amber light, the sun
stares beneath the limbs of trees aflame
again. And from long, crisp shadows,

a few wild gods dance with winter's chill.
No call for calendars when every canyon
rings with the bellows of bulls looking

for work, or a fight, reducing fences to
barbed wire nightmares, splintered posts
with long excavations either side of tangles.

During nights of no moon, the big talk fires
testosterone and fence repair, purpose here
as the sweet fragrance of cows fills the air.

FINDING HOME

1.
Packed mules all-summer of '66,
either side of the Kaweahs,
over Franklin, over Blackrock

leading a string along the sandy track
between the steep scree and beaver dams
at Upper Funston, anytime in my mind —

> gentle thud of hooves behind me,
> long strides rubbing loads and leather,
> jingle of snaps on loose draw chains —

my ears were eyes. Sometimes
you could feel the beasts inhale
before the ropes got tight, before

the story you hoped to tell exploded.
But here an excited calm collects and
glides with rainbow trout in clear pools

beavers made — here God takes
His vacation away from the phone and
leaves desperate prayers to angels.

2.
USC after Watts was surreal —
young women in crinoline, kegs
of beer, everywhere — a little

world lost in the black
asphalt and concrete, a long
day's ride to earth left alone.

Before the war and the Sixties
came down hard, we'd slip off
to the Ashgrove on Melrose,

displaced country boys
listening for a little bit of home —
John Hammond, Lightening

Hopkins, Ramblin' Jack
on stage, two dollar ticket,
four dollar cover, two

drinks served before the show —
and Jack is young, forty-four
years ago. Hat, boots and acoustic

ready to jump off stage and whip
the usher interrupting '912 Greens' —
he hollers instead, 'Hold that gate!'

BLUE MOON

Started the fire at 3:15

>   *Western Livestock Journal*
>   and broken fencepost
>   split thin redwood kindling,
>   oak and manzanita —

and left upstream
        after spraying weeds all day
        with the *Kawasaki Mule*

                feed on one side of the wire,
                weeds on the other —

to check on the neighbor
just out of the hospital,
        too sore to 'rock 'n roll'
        New Year's Eve.

Shared a glass of whiskey wishes
and listened to the girls talk cattle,
bulls and marbling.

You and I back home alone
red wine around the fire, meat on
when the moon cleared the saddle
        this side of Sulphur

                top sirloins,
                garlic cloves
                        oiled in tin foil
                licked by flames

under a remnant storm sheet —
        silver cloud reflection
        aiming higher westerly,

          big bright moon in the V

     filigreed by silk oak leaves
     dry and hanging like feathers

until the meat was done.

GARDEN JOURNAL, APRIL 2011

Ongoing war, the spring campaign
to save the seedlings — more cotyledons
felled atop the soft, damp ridge
of well-worked soil under last night's moon,
new cucumbers grown pale and limp —
heavy little hands curl helplessly
in gray light. With war chants, you shake
the last of the bird-friendly, thirty-dollar jug
of *Sluggo* into the yellow Iris spears,
abbreviated epithets slung with another
shell upon the ground made sure underfoot.
Combing rake-like, your fingers drag
through broad green leaves, looking
for the enemy and pink casualties to save —
strawberries hollowed before ripe. Even
the volunteer Sunflowers have been attacked.

The garden,
        our ticket to postponing town,
exhales, exasperates new law —
        I imagine the machete
        clinched between my rounded crowns,
air thick as battle smoke,
as every living thing knows, even
the oriole, brightly singing for a mate
to help weave and sling a sock nest
in the Palo Verde near the cherry tree,
can feel the uneasy certainty of a new régime.

We sharecrop our cultivated world
of few straight rows, snow peas reaching
beyond support to bloom and drip
from a round and rusty water trough,
potatoes in another, as asparagus dares to bolt.

Drawn from leafy cover to pie pans of beer,
we entertain the snails, and ourselves
with red wine glee, lopsided shells too heavy
to slime a straight line to dark safety.

LIVING A DREAM

The same naked trek into first light
as you sleep, my sound of heel upon
a wooden floor for fresh shirt and socks—

all the possibilities of a day's work align
with the necessity of trying to stay ahead
of trouble, breaking trail for tomorrow.

We paint by day, small strokes now, details
that can be washed away in a heartbeat,
in a storm, in the unlikely, despite the joy

of being able. How I wish I'd known
when I was young and hard that this
was it, that we could make it true.

OUR TIME

There is no mistake that we are here
to work together, to hold the fragile in
abeyance and focus on routines we know —

to care with sure and calloused hands
and sort unspoken grief to unseen pens
to haul home like our own stray cattle

when it's done. Scattered by distance
apart from the world and its tragic
consequences — its sad ambitions

and addictions — we come to celebrate
and revere our skills with the unpredictable
and rise to persevere as one. Sometimes

the heart, or is it the soul that shudders,
or is it the moon at its perigee that pulls
emotions up like swirling tides around us

that we dare not speak for fear of hearing
our own voice quake? Is it age worn thin?
We work around raw and tender parts,

find new ways to hold our rope and rein
until time heals the hole in each of us —
neighbors for a long time — it is our time.

for Kenny & Virginia

WITH YOU

> *At night make me one with the darkness.*
> *In the morning make me one with the light.*
> -Wendell Berry ("Prayers and
> Sayings of the Mad Farmer")

In time, we will give into dreamless sleep,
rest with the dust and debris of other lives,
within the comfort and compost of grand trees,

eventually. One earth, the fertile dirt awaiting
seed, and rain, and with the sun's pull upward,
the possibility of fruit — let me be one leaf

open at dawn, let these old knees find grace,
impaired ears the tune. One last slow dance
with you among the shadows of the moon.

for Robbin

IF WE HAVE LOVE

Thatched and lashed with horsehair
thread, even well-built nests
have casualties, tip in a storm,

spill family overboard, and we
remain to make repairs—find reason,
where so often there is none.

If we have love, we have no choice
but to fall with them, over and over
into the void—and we do it,

not to savor grief, but to collect
what parts we can, to piece our nest
back-together again.

for Jeff and Alie

VALENTINE

She woke on the edge of a clear stream and made her way to a mansion built on pillars of gold, whose silver walls glowed like a lantern in the sun. She ventured inside to find floors of precious stones, rooms of treasure and art, and comforting voices that she could hear but not see that invited her to dine, to bathe, to sleep, and to enjoy every imaginable comfort. She fell asleep to a chorus of angels, accompanied by a harp.

        – Teresa Jordan, ("Cupid: The Soap Opera")

'Tis Cupid come in darkness
to dance in dreams, dear Psyche—
how we yearn like children

to unlock deep chests,
to comfort and confirm
our richest vulnerabilities,

our nakedness in the light.
O' to be so simply mortal
is the envy of all the gods!

IN CASE OF PEACE

One could say there is no peace,
never peace everywhere on earth—

some become soldiers, well-honed
tools of the powerful and afraid,
of the unreasonable, of the inhumane
in each of us—and some become

what they must to survive them.
Some become prey, feed and fodder
for the stronger, and the rest of us
become many feet on the treadmill.

But there are moments, epiphanies
lurking and waiting to spring
and spread wide and feathered wings
around us. We must slow down

to be caught, we must be watchful,
learn their track and sign, know
their scent and become familiar
with where they haunt the wild.

And when they find us, stretch
the senses and forget ourselves.

TOWARDS FALL

1.

Off the hill behind the house, their home
since spring, sleek black heifers mill about
from under trees upon bleached feed

come evening. Talk around the trough
is brief with easy gestures, expectant mothers
fill with water, graze lazily and wait.

Together since calves, they mirror change
and remember in gazes — fire within
as they move, chatting idly about nothing.

2.

A coyote crosses in the distance,
not unseen as pups upcanyon practice
yips and yodeling. Lichened boulders

hold to the mountain, fractured stacks
of granite waiting for the decade, the
century to let go. A trail of baby quail

stir the dust, a gray hawk's quiet glide
between oaks. Easy voices on the road
peddle down the creek towards home.

3.

And the dark swallows all. Tonight
lying naked in our bed exposed
to the sweet breath of a mowed lawn

upon our skins, to all the sounds
outside that find a part to play
in dreams, we close our eyes and

trust in the dog's bark, the cow's
bawl and the sun's hot passion
to come and go again 'til gone.

UNDER OAKS

It comes to me only now
with roots too deep to be
transplanted without shock,
        that I wear the dust
        of where I've been
        upon my flesh
        and in my lungs
already — we are the one clod
that we inhabit and nurture
through drought, flood and time.

It comes to me only now
that we have worked quite well
together, our ebb and flow
        allowances as
        longtime lovers
        learn that they
        are part of the same
landscape — this fold of dirt
where the shine from ice on granite
is honeycombed with holes.

It comes to me only now
that time is short for natives
unless you are an oak
        making shade and acorns
        for the future,
        adding more than
        you take away
from this earth — this tilted plain
of clay and rock — sacred places
under oaks where we can talk.

WILD WORDS

Somewhere you are dying, a path crossed,
remembered and lost—sweet moments sculpted,
an innocence now seasoned with perspective

from other places. We did not know it,
did not believe the obvious,
and did not care what others thought.

More like fish than the mast lights of ships
passing on an empty sea, more like swimming
parallel for awhile in a current of our own

making. Will you remember when you wonder
on your death bed, when you are tired of life,
and will you smile at all the things we said?

Not every face has a name anymore, some
I'll never forget. But we stirred the waters
with words, wild words, for a moment.

IT

We can call it anything we want,
anytime, anywhere in whispers —
chins tucked under our breaths.

We can pray to oak trees and rocks,
bless spring seeps and marvel
with maroon skies before the flood

of deadfall measures the creek bank.
We can set free whatever words we want,
quietly — and it should be enough.

Common Tongue

...we *who must turn*
everything to words while they, so alive
need so few to speak their loves.
- Keith Wilson
("The Streets of San Miguel")

COMMON TONGUE

We know them by name
or short description—cattle,
horses, dogs and people—

trees, rocks and springs,
peaks, flats and creeks,
and the trails we found

to find them. Natives
notice details, our every
quirk and give us names

as well. An abbreviated
language, spoken mostly
with motion and what's

on our mind. No one
wants trouble with so
much going-on outside.

MOUNTAIN RIVER

I reach for a cold river to feel its urgency—
my esoteric metaphor for the force within
life off the flat ground, believing Newton
surrendered to numbers to quantify

the forces that drive us, the elastic thread
that tugs and stretches, floods and trickles
ever off the mountain where trees reach
desperately from the depths of well-worn

canyons, pine and cedar, smooth boulders
under the guttural roar of waterfalls, deep
pools, riffles of fish with water ouzels
skipping upstream—to feel rejuvenated.

for JEG

A. M. DREAMS

Summer dawn, wild oats blond,
they wake from dreams beyond
ridgeline silhouettes and think

of me, or someone like me
with sweet alfalfa leaf—young cows
to be, their flesh fills, springs

pink around me and I am pleased.
They feel it as I move through
our congregation on this hillside.

The road below fills with pickups
towing toys, the purr of hopped-up
four-wheel drives, tents and trailers

like blood pumped into the mountains
where snowmelt leaks and tumbles
into treacherous streams, rivers

hungry for adventurous ignorance—
her breasts heave. These girls and I
have closed that other world away

and speak to the moment, study
one another's movement. I dream
of them, and them of me.

CLOUD WAVES

Forecasts vary, computer models change:
dry rain of fiery leaves, stirred and torn
from the honey locust tree, cloud waves

in all shades of gray — a dark flotilla
peeks over the ridge for ships run aground
against the Sierras leaking cargo low

on Blue Ridge trimmed with a white ribbon.
We sip whiskey, replay the week and squeal
like children on each gust, tip our glasses

to the work got done. To herds of virgins
readied for the Wagyu bulls, gentle ladies
churning under a full moon. To the mothers

with first calves driven up canyon, now
grazing the north slopes as it tries to rain.
To the four we couldn't find by day:

awakened by their bawling for babies,
night lit by the moon, they awaited
dawn at the gate while we slept easily.

DOCS NO SOX   1666851
March 21, 1980 – June 4, 2010

Filling the hole—covering the other half
of the dance that blessed uneven ground
and unforgiving circumstance with heart

and elegance—took time, each scoop spilled
and built around your crimson rose petals,
garden yarrow ripening beside a bouquet

of purple brodiaea wound with pink centaury.
Domestic and wild, the mystic and suddenly
symbolic branded in brilliant colors savored

between each bucketful until the last full
moment was eclipsed with dark, damp earth.
It took time to find and feel hydraulic grace,

smooth and efficient gestures of respect
for the horse you groomed beneath the blue
oaks with dear words, a bucket of oats,

show sheen and fly spray on softest hair,
his forelock finally full. And as you waited
for the vet, the atrophied old man followed

to the lone oak shade near the open hole—
souls making promises on a cool breeze,
one last walk to the bottom of all things.

YEAR OF THE ACORN

A short and easy fall between
summer and winter, oak trees
heavy, woodpeckers overstocked

for cold, every crack and post
full, a left over crop drops
in circles beneath the trees.

Briefly disrupted, coveys of quail
return to bob upon ripe, black
mats crushed along the back roads.

Dark rafts of wild pigeons
rake the sky between the ridges,
deer fat and blue. It seems easy

to adapt to plenty, larders of pocket
gophers packed and planted
for spring, dry oak and manzanita

stacked beneath the eaves. Like hawks
sequestered to leaves when it rains,
we're ready for almost anything.

PLODDING

Even the sleek, young cows
like having time to think, more
willing to help get the job done
to stay awhile longer
in these hills—the sort is easy.

Except for a single set of tracks
through the dew on new green,
first light glints, each blade afire
and twinkling like starlight
to turn the world on its head,

to stop the clock and pause
for a breath or two, for the flesh
to ingest, for a glimpse
in this poem for going slow—
an unfinished noun, like home,

like the Kaweah peaks dressing
and undressing snow, each sheet
slipping downstream a little,
revealing granite, or stripped
at once to flood—we never know

what is yet left to see of wild
extremes, of truth, of natural
beauty — *the sole business of
poetry*—before we go. Even
cows like having time to think.

SNAKES IN THE ROAD

Like steel-jawed traps slightly buried
and camouflaged with leaves and grass —
like land mines half-way 'round the world,

we step around them, waiting
for the old horse or dog on the edge
of suffering, or the crippled cow,

before pulling the necessary trigger.
We cannot pretend we do not see
gophers in the garden, the endless trail

of ants, the rats' nest — we deal death
as we wait for our own, always hoping
our compassion might outweigh the facts.

Killing is not for old men who have lost
their focus, who cannot pull the blinders up
to eclipse themselves. A man can endure

only so many squeezes, so many crosshairs
before he begins to step around insects
and spiders, avoiding the snakes in the road.

COWBOY POEM

They think, see you carefully and read
your simple poetry as if an open window
to your mind. You must offer honesty,

kindly, find your rhythm on a hillside,
find grace and patience where there is
no hiding your intent so far away

from the corrals. This morning's page:
steep—Blue Oaks thick on a north slope
slick and rocky where the grass has held

and drawn them, peppered dots of cows
and calves appear and disappear within
a raft of trees where they should be,

despite your sort of wets and drys,
despite the pens and alleys you try
to write around—they are content.

HEIFERS

It is their faces, I remember,
heavy with calf, deep and careful
looks from questioning dark eyes
circled around me as I counted
walking, standing among them,
still — making our twice-a-day
ritual easy, visiting to inspect
loose progress without the hay.

Their tag numbers are familiar
rhymes from clipboard paper,
disconnected dates and notes
that may be useful someday —
but now it is their faces
I remember in this pasture
lazing before us, their first
fat calves soon to be weaned.

Drawn with evening close
to the house, to my loud
conversation tossed at gods
who understand, to you moving
in the garden, changing water,
picking strawberries, we are
comforted like family
brought back together again.

Generations out of poison oak
and fractured granite come
to us now. There are other worlds
with good fortune, other ways
to feel important, but none come
so willingly out of the wild
with such trust, just to say hello
or follow wherever we go.

BULLS

Two tons, heads still locked
after the three mile drive
of cows and calves was done,

swirling bellows and dust
left behind to settle possession
of what was gone —

flat constant contact,
pole to nose, black silhouettes
standing exhausted alone.

It took a week
before they could see —
blind testosterone.

SPRING FEVER

A little left where they spent
time in the car in front of the gate
last night, smoked Marlboros,

ate pork rinds, drank half-dozen
Budweisers out of town,
away from home, when she

leaned against the fence
to look up at the stars, padding
the sand in and the dust up

with bare, little feet — talking
as he dropped empty sunflower
seeds between his own.

They made love, I'd guess,
in the matted grass —
the coyotes howled for free.

FIRST AT THE GATE

Trying to meet me, eye-to-eye,
the old Red horse wants to go—
not knowing where, or how long

like the Bay horse years ago,
left behind the first time: gallop,
stop and turn on the fence

for an hour on his own, within
earshot of cows and calves
bawling at the branding with

old friends and neighbors
down the road—time takes us
all for a ride. Shed, grow winter

hair, play before the gusty storms,
they have no fear of the end,
nothing other than grand purpose

now. "But after awhile," my Dad
once said, "you have to get used
to not being first in line."

BONE TO PICK

A post, a fence — little evidence
of generations grazing steep
chemise and fractured granite,

snow flats and sage, in that other
realm of wild rules — the raven rests
to compose his next poem, his next

creative exercise to badger and pester
the nature of whatever happens by, and
perhaps, feed himself at the same time.

No saintly aspirations, nothing
memorized — he'll stalk a newborn
calf by dancing to nursery rhymes,

looking to pluck out an eye. Quick
study, he reads motion and mind
and mimics us all, chortling in flight.

CALVING FIELDS

Blond on black,

a filigree of empty shells on long stems bent
to new life trembling in a breeze, the light
and hollow grace of late spring rains, these

wild oats arched, these sun-bleached skeletons
that remain, concealing the first throbs of heart
driven by instinct apart from the cowherd.

Sometimes we cannot see, cannot find
what she has hidden, despite curious coyote
pups skulking in the shade, ravens in trees.

Sometimes we miss the miracle of cycles,
the circles of rain — think each day the same.
These old hills come alive, inhale in long

shadows of oaks shedding leaves and acorns.
The invitations have been sent, bulk mail
on gusts to everyone, but only the wild respond.

ASK A CALF

We are born to see the light.
Ask the new calf this morning
early, after its first day

of incessant licking while
wobbling along her belly,
to nose the warm bag

swelling with nourishment,
just to close its eyes
when put to bed that first time —

back into that blackness
safe between a fallen limb
and the trunk of an oak tree.

Everything is new and disconnected
when its eyes open again
to see what it smells

or stumbles over, listening
for a voice, always known,
to find her beautiful.

NOVEMBER

There are times to edit, summarize—
close chapters and move towards
some purpose for the words, rise

with the sun and let syllables float
across the colored pool and through
its rain of leaves—all that I wrote

baked behind me, November, alive
like spring. We are winter people
grazing changes as they arrive

from the endless black and blue
sky. We pause to look up, wish
and pray, find gods to tip glasses to—

we are oaks with acorns at our feet,
long-limbed sycamores dancing naked
in the rain—no time to be discrete.

OPEN

Sweet conjecture,
that plane of possibility
between earth and sky,

a space that speaks
a common language
with the eyes

recording reaction,
replaying surprise
without words, yet

we try painting
moments, matching
colors, so as not to forget,

blending sounds
into a song
to carry in our heads —

small reminders
to hang in the hall
like windows open.

TREE FROG MOMENT

We have come to this, now — this place,
wherever sheltered, this point in time
rushing towards us like a locomotive —

when the conclusion of all things rests
in one long moment if we're lucky
watching the tree frog explore its territory.

We have learned to shut the hawkers out,
banging their wares in the alley, the needy
politicians with puppy eyes, and the orators —

all of them pushed to the dusty corners
of this moment on someone else's landscape
for over sixty-five million years.

Waiting to be Served

Never weep. Let them play,
Old violence is not too old to beget new values.
                    - Robinson Jeffers ("The Bloody Sire")

WAITING TO BE SERVED

*Everyone praises a different day
but few know their nature.*
　　　　　　- Hesiod ("Works and Days")

Today, the world changes — too many people
leaning towards the north star has tipped the planet,
exposing shadow beneath the tree that we believed
would comfort us and always bear fruit.

Yes, we are the centerpiece of that myth,
adding the last bit of gold thread to the fabric
that comes untrue, unraveling and fading
in the relentless, everlasting look of the sun.

Now I can remember, replay the finer details
from a distance, see myself among the mindless,
shoulder-to-shoulder in the crowding alleys
pressed onward towards the mounted silhouettes

in the sunset. But a corral board broke early-on,
around Vietnam. The sky was clearer then,
more obvious and less complicated, not everyone
leaned in the same direction, waiting to be served.

AT THE HEART OF THINGS

> *A rattlesnake coils among cold stones,*
> *full of mice, waits for evening*
> *when he will hunt again.*
> > - Linda M. Hasselstrom ("Morning
> > News on Windbreak Road")

No feast on Dry Creek, no dance among the trees –
no amount of words rhymed with earth will change
the arrogance of men primping in the light.

We do not breathe by their generosity, nor believe
they may, someday, be gods — saviors of a nation
always at war with what it can't comprehend.

We have forgotten, perhaps we never heard
the silent mantra of the harvest strum in our heads –
hands busy, bodies bent, genuflecting in the dirt.

Or been of a tribe of men, women and communities
that still rise to raise a glass to that great expanse
that feeds us all we need, sparingly. Riding out

alone, do you remember conversations with living
and dead? Did you mark the granite outcrop,
hang words in an oak tree, or just let them loose

on a hawk's wing? If only Jeffer's perch-mates,
power and desire — not greed — might roost in
Washington, we'd dedicate his fountain to humanity.

STYX AND STONES

Darkness sneaks-up outside to surround the house
engulfing the pasture of Angus heifers with fresh
black calves curled beside them, merging oaks

and sycamores along the creek with sculpted ridges
flexed and thrusting the spearhead of Sulphur
towards a rusty bucket sky leaking promises of light.

But in between, Cerebus waits and watches
with underworld hobgoblins picking their teeth
with redwood posts and flossing with barbed wire

while we say our prayers. Somewhere in the blackness
south, a climax of coyote yips is answered north,
here and there, then closer west to work the canyon

into a frenzy spilling fear into every crack of logic.
No one knows what's out there! — what dark forces
scramble from out of the bowels of Hades.

TO HELL IN A HANDBASKET

We have these conversations, you and I,
about those spawned after the world was
saved —
　　　back when Rosie left the factory
　　　and some of the men came home

heroes. We had our war — remember
what it cost? And before that, Crazy K
shipping missiles to Cuba, JFK

shot down in Dallas, Bobby in L.A,
MLK in Memphis on my birthday?
Conspiracies or the crazed among us

driven by something that will not die,
that fearful and dissatisfied undercurrent
we nurture, turn commercial, profit by.

Hear the hatred rattling in the grass?
Old war babies crying in their sleep, still
believing they have had a say and glad

to have a black man now to blame. Bad
times, hard times, yes — but we've seen
worse immersed in self — gratification.

The rock doesn't care anymore, rivers
laugh off the mountains, but the deserts
remember every word in our heads,

every conversation wishing more — just
to find a way to keep the wagon moving
without the weight of hate.

EQUILIBRIUM

Off the mountain, the stone turns round —
sheds it edges and rests between pools,
between trees, between the floods

with nothing left to prove. It has not
taken long to fall from steep ideals,
far peaks like teeth tearing at the sky.

A steady roar of news pushes upstream,
ruffling willows, oaks and sycamores,
yet much is lost along the way here —

like the petty and picayune that don't
sell much for long, or the slow drums
of the ever-fearful souls determined

that the world has gone to hell with hate.
What genius lets these molten fires explode,
leak out to cool beneath the ice, to create

these ever-changing clouds of steam
at Eyjafjallajokull? And we so pleased
that it's not the end of a work in progress.

MORE

*In the name of more we destroy
for coal the mountain and its forest
and so choose the insatiable flame.*
- Wendell Berry ("2008")*

It is the lazy nature of our dreams, wanting
that which we conceive — we float on lakes rising
while islands sink, despite repeated dawnings

and better sense. The hawk remodels his high nest
of twigs when the leaves come, refines efficiency
with practice — talon and beak to soar and feed

generations. He has his place in sycamores
along the creek — a Red Tail pair, chests bared
to winter sun when we hay horses waiting.

Do they, from the cold, bare branch, dream
of warm domesticity and dependence, a store
of gophers or wealth of squirrels, or do they

find us curious? The blueprints and templates
to gather plenty have endured, yet we feed
our future to the insatiable flame in our mind.

OLD SCHOOL

Ideals, so simple, in that slice of time
war babies were hatched, Rockwellesque
imprints that don't fit the hydra-headed,

loose ends of our contemporary minds
looking for the quick and convenient,
something new to do. No old hats left

to wear outside, no black or white
designations, even the Snidelys have
shaved the look in their eyes. It is easy

to wander off to work alone, let the mind go
to make its fortune, to face the Herculean
with golden sword, red kerchief slung

with enough for the long way back
renewed, with something done — a living
art within the shell of the more mundane.

USURA – CONTRA NATURA

> *with usura*
> *hath no man a painted paradise on his church wall*
> - Ezra Pound ("With Usura" Canto XLV)

Bent beside furrows like rivers boiling
from beneath the skirts of the first orange
tree, we set free regattas of twigs and leaves,

before mud-dams rechanneled our father's water
for scrap, two-by-four barges hauling freight.
We explored cobwebbed corners of the barn,

played pretend aboard dusty wagon seats,
took turns driving winged steeds into
dancing particles afloat in the splintered

sunbeams. Flame in the cave, our shadows
flicker on the wall, dancing like cathedral
angels from paradise — the places we shape

beyond the grasp of governments and time,
beyond the baited traps of the same insatiable
perchmates: Mrs. Greed and Mr. Power.

WITHOUT A DIME

Another game in the backroom, smoke
clouds a swinging lamp, wagers made
'for' and 'against' the whims of human nature
as dancing girls serve, and serve again

all over town for a dollar. We could be
the carcass on the table, flesh sliced thin,
honed steel a glint, they toil and angle
like bloody butchers trimming the best cuts

for themselves. Outside, pimps and barkers
watch the door, up and down the street,
pretend to be selective, pocket bribes
and whisper, 'it's the safest game in town.'

No tea cups here, no cloth napkins,
no silver candelabras holding flame —
the play is fast and furious, full of
promises, 'you'll never leave the same.'

Always gambling on the sunlight, on
the rain, the planet spins its own roulette:
hawks glide and rivers murmur to the wild
that's left without a dime to its name.

WINTER'S ECSTASY

The old granite forgets half a year's filth...
- Robinson Jeffers ("November Surf")

The sweep of leaves, the track erased,
first winter storm — spring's discarded
petals, summer's seed, and September's

discontent raked into the earth await
Pacific passion from whence we've come
to rely upon — it pumps in arteries.

Even the old veins swell with anticipation,
dry flesh craving streams, runoff flushed
in rivulets, old slate clean again, the only

promise that may bear fruit despite the lies
of men. Her scent upon wind gusts,
we prepare and pray for rare extremes:

all the damp furies inhaled, the sweet
smell of storm, and after-rain of molding
green. We renew our vows and begin again.

A GUST

I can say it now, tell the truth of how
a gust can turn a leaf, a life, a phrase —
we cannot claim these things that move

us, any more than we can own the moon
despite our investment since children
searching its fullness for a face in the dark.

Some gods are dependable, arrive on time:
thick oaks and granite rooted in this earth.
But most are illusive and walk the edge

of our senses, talk logic without words
we think we understand. It is enough
to be among them, watching, listening

to what can't be captured, what won't fit
in a colored box to be labeled and sold
like puffed wheat, like politics and religion.

SULPHUR SYCAMORE

Grown up where they can,
each reaches for light and water
in the canyon rock and sand,

drinking deeply to lose limbs
they can't support, trying to tell us
the same thing, over and over again.

We are not the only species flawed
with big ideas—it's normal, it's natural
to keep on like we had a brain.

THIS SIDE OF SKY

Light comes round, shapes hills with shadow,
gilds the faces of tilted peaks, pyramids upcanyon
where gods must live to stay clear of the clatter —

ridge after ridge afire upon the green this side of sky
like a loose deck at dawn, glimpses of kings, queens
and knaves in the deal. O' how my father cringed

with my selected verse, one-sided, loose leaves
bound under a clear plastic cover in limited editions
published by Xerox in the 60s — that first trip

and stumble into small press, Everyman's magic
for a dime-a-copy. I liked the look, but his reviews,
couched and pillowed between long breaths,

did not deter nor inspire me, though troubled him
as perhaps it should have in those days of Republicans
and young men in a long jungle war. Say good-bye

to the Draft, the sword, become the disambiguation
of governments, we have evolved to mercenaries
and drones, there are no kids to mow our lawns —

clean-cut, grown-ups now, running for offices.
He would be happy with my pastoral imagery,
lift an eye, grin a little at the pantheistic,

yet remembering when he drug me out of bed,
by the foot, to show me the Kaweah steaming
among cottonwoods, a colored mist rising.

                              for David Wilke

NINE-ELEVEN, ELEVEN

Gray and purple dawn, broken clouds,
thin edges lit ash-white press heavily
from the outside — beyond the bear

and coyote collecting tax along the creek,
cleaning-up and taking shares of new life,
feeding on the hapless and innocent

lying flat in the grass. This air is thick
with fear, fetid breath held too long
circling the planet, creating its own

climate of thunder and fire. No perfect
world without predators and casualties —
without the friction of nature's humans.

IN SELF-DEFENSE

Easy to get emotional on the Senate floor, misspeak
extemporaneously to take the snipers' potshots while
trying to save the arts for humanity like a little girl lost

in the crossfire, or before investing more on war.
Katrina came and left New Orleans underwater
slick with oil. New England fracks for natural gas

and Fukoshima leaks real radioactivity to California's
happy cows. Still hungry for energy, it's difficult
to live in the moment, as we wear ever-changing fear

and panic like uncomfortable underclothes, like
sackcloth. On the surface, we exchange living green
for speed and comfort, swap our aching knees and

yesterday's horses for more horsepower mid-stream,
planting houses in the San Joaquin that used to feed
a more patient population. The sun will dawn despite

our hopeless battle with the clock, despite the weight
of addictions we can't escape—I write in self-defense
as if there were only moments left to live, one at a time.

for Harry Reid

ECONOMICS

My father plied economics
to everything—cows, feed
and even rain, hoping

his demand for wonder
might supply it. Greenheads
rising from the cattails,

sunrise cut and streaked
into separate beams
by Sawtooth and the Kaweahs,

he looked for God beyond
the numbers, and saw
enough to be disappointed

in mankind. He spared
our living with his being
right in ninety-seven,

spared the politicians
written lectures, and left
to watch the show —

forever assured
that no tree grows
to the sky.

HAWK & CROW

Rock is always right

despite deepening fissures, despite
debates twixt hawk and crow
for its highest outcrop,
      for a foothold
      with each squawk
      of myopic politique
      barked in the wind
      as they fly.

Eagles care less, egrets
go fishing and watch the sky
over soft, white shoulders —
      quail post sentries
and all the little birds stay busy
collecting twigs and string
to make their nests.

      No one really listens, only
      the angry looking to blame
      someone beyond the mirror

for all these changes now
that nothing stays the same
in this costly economy
of comfort and convenience,

      despite information
      at lightening speeds,
      hawk and crow
      have no answers

they just like to fight.

RETURN

A little too abstract, a little to wise,
It is time for us to kiss the earth again.
                    - Robinson Jeffers ("Return")

We may not have the currency
to invest anymore, now that town
has rebooted our minds, changed

the circuitry, on feed in Fat City,
right off I-5. Not even a glance up
at the smooth Coalinga Hills

to graze old times, find a canyon
to get lost in. We may be too
well-bred to return and get by.

YELLOW SLICKERS

We will always be suspect
no matter how much hay
we intend to feed, pickup

dripping loose alfalfa once
the strings are cut, always one
nervous on the periphery,

sensing something
from another plane
when our eyes meet.

Was it a forgotten stray
thought she found out
grazing, some unfinished

poem abandoned,
misunderstood, misheard
in the rhyming?

Or did I get close
to speaking her language—
closer than she to ever taste

the first fluffy bites
of joy and satisfaction?
So much like people

who wear their fears
like yellow slickers
always ready for a storm.

CRITES LAKE

...we walk the bottom of an ocean we call sky.
          - Jim Harrison ("River II")

It is our nature to believe in more
beyond the surface — though we toil
for plenty here upon the ocean's floor,

a hierarchy of bottom fish, both slim
and fat — wanting to believe in something
more attainable to all, a free place

for the spirit to try its wings in the light,
beyond the murky depths shadowed by
darker silhouettes of sharks and whales.

How deep the sky! Unnamed on maps,
near Coyote Pass, 10,000 feet above it all,
'CRITES LAKE' perforated with an ice pick

in the tin, square bottom of a five-gallon can
placed near the outlet jammed with dark
green backs of rainbow trout, spawning,

every one a pound or more in those days.
Just before the moon rose and the granite
glowed like a lantern, there seemed no end

to the stars — far, tiny bubbles glinting
near the surface, our passenger jets
and sputniks streaking beneath them.

SIDESHOW

Like try-outs for the lead,

      it's hard to tell
      who's not acting,
      who's not for real.

      This cream risen:
      American prime
      hoofing down

      the campaign trail —
      another year
      of non-sequitur,

      closet embarrassments,
      and hateful insults
      to endure. Bad karma

      for hard times, we hope
      who pulls the strings
      does not lose interest

in the play.

I WONDER

if technology
is like a drug
or glass of red craved

when the light is right, if
cell phones should be
sewn under the skin

like pacemakers
for the brain, or is it
a weapon like a gun,

better than a rock or club
to wave up-close,
or is it how we keep

our space intact, yet
safely connected
to an insane world?

Are we truly any closer to
understanding one another—
or ourselves, or the dirt

we are nurtured by
and will return to
when the light is right—

where shadows dance
beyond a ring of stones
and man-made magic?

Out of Doors

Forgive the hymn, friend. Out of doors
it doesn't count as praying.
> *- Quinton Duval ("One Bright Morning")*

OUT OF DOORS

It may be hours before a word escapes
my mouth across the creek, through
half-a-dozen gates latched behind me

like pairs of quail disturbed for a moment —
over snake tracks and caravans of ants
beneath the inquisitive wing of a Red Tail.

Suddenly, I hear my voice come from
the outside in, a gravelly phrase added
to conclude the conversation in my head.

I have to laugh at my reply in the same voice
before one of us cuts it short — like making
ugly faces, it could be habit forming,

so addictive that I might forever stay
praying like crazy in the wilderness,
talking to cattle and animals, to twisted

trees, perfect springs, ever-seeping — all
who say lots of things these days, as if they
knew something — and someone's got to listen.

IN THE LAND OF AWE

These lakes and cliffs
still remember me
            - Norman Schaefer ("Upper Basin")

Imagine the people they have known —
feet felt slipping in the scree, the dreams
released within the reflected light of stars

off granite, near the top of the world.
The air is thin, the Milky Way a smear.
Time is kind, it wears so slowly

that each peak is a monument to young
memory etched upon its face, interred
here. Awesome! to be so well known.

> *You recognize me,*
> *you entice me tenderly.*
> — Hermann Hesse ("Spring")

...and I fall within
a new skin of limbs,
tender leaves and bloom —

while fog enshrouds
the naked dance
of sycamores in the creek

and late snow clings
to the green grass
on Sulphur Peak.

You are a strong woman
and I am weak within
this tapestry, this fine weave —

each thread alive, binding
cinching and relieved
to have me rest upon it.

JUST RIGHT!

Scrambling through loose rocks
On an old trail
All of a summer's day.
                    - Gary Snyder ("Milton by Firelight")

What better place to read
than by firelight, each word
flickering into the next.

Slow progress in the harsh
landscapes of our mind's
eye, to linger there and read

Snyder aloud to friends
around white coals, shadows
and sound, starlit night.

It happens then, the wind
in pines, off edges of granite,
the bell mare and coyote

interrupting lines,
feeling poetic
just at the right time.

CEDAR GROVE

Within walls of bare rock, no urgency
to improve the moment, no cell phone call
for plastic gadgets to hold us connected—

thin swirl of smoke, black and blue
coffeepot, wine jug passed—enough
and all we need to please our gods

circled 'round the fire. From the ash
of a hundred years exposed, pine needles
and cedar cones piled for banked coals,

they have risen from this midden since
we were children—fathers and grandfathers
buried beneath our feet, free of the flat

dreams farmed with this slow snowmelt
leaking, slipping and dripping into the roar
and foam of the *Rio de los Santos Reyes*,

of the Kings, wearing cold granite smooth
that dares and intimidates the soul—cures
the sinful and the satisfied with elsewhere.

BEGINNING OF A SCREEN PLAY

The scene opens around a fire,
shadows of huddled men dancing
to white coals stirred for another chunk
of tamarack, bell mare grazing
distant darkness by granite starlight,
sweet and damp in her nostrils,
to the snowmelt's murmur
leaking down into another world.

You are there among them now,
young and listening in thin night air,
following a herd of horses from
Cuyama up the Kern, over Farewell
to the miners in Mineral King
by yourself at seventeen — Onus Brown.

If lucky, you may be a story only,
a far-fetched tale of discarded truth —
short chapters of wild accomplishment
that will not matter in the future,
but for the embellished retelling.

The camera zooms into eyes a glint
beneath your brim, cigarette inhaled,
jug tipped, passed and burning still —

nothing worse among these men,
than to have nothing left to tell.

FIVE HUNDRED SOULS

I am here to gather cattle, ride the ridges,
see — light step on the morning, rising
higher before the sun shatters atop Broke-Up
to search out darkness in the draws.

Soft dirt under hoof, cowtrails cut in grass
on grade travel easy to the same places,
speak no tracks yet today. The Coyote Tree
is dying, lost the limbs they hung them on

in the old days, my young days when
this was the way — old road the CCCs
with wheelbarrows, pick and shovel,
mule-drawn Fresno scraper in the hands

of many men carved upwards out of Greasy
where it met the Kaweah before the lake,
the dam, before the lowland changed.
Wide sand beach with tules, cattail-hemmed

Wukchumne camp, five hundred souls
before me. I was afraid, dark within
Chiishe's den in Belle Point's flank.
Hear my father say, 'Keep your eyes peeled!'

I am here to gather cattle, ride the day
down — cows, calves and a century and a half
spread before me — the buck and run of years
that haven't changed, still shaping me.

for Hank

AMONG US

Almost invisible, these gods
are not immortal, not
the all-powerful deities

displayed for symbols
and slogans — some haven't even
a name to trade your mind

and heart for, like in heaven,
where pouting angels
look down with envy

upon their pagan games.
These gods slip upon you
around a flame, surround

like darkness, touch your
shoulder, or cover the flesh
in a dry rain of oak leaves —

they breathe the memories
of all that's gone before —
living secretly among us.

ANYMAN

The jokes come snowmelt easy,
off the Rubies, cloudy runoff rising
down the South Fork as we grin
into wind gusts like pickup pups,
slit-eyes watering in a light rain.

> I haven't time to trace
> how I found my way
> to this strange country —
> under sea undulations
> with dirt road ruts
> forking in the thatches
> of willows swelling with bud,
> where naked cottonwoods play
> dead along the bottoms
> of the high desert in May.

A quick language of quips, unrefined
and unfinished sentences sprinkled
with double-entendres, flashing eyes
locking, laughing just long enough
to chase the cold river downstream.

No longer lean boys looking for adventure,
we raise families to respect fate, to find
their rhythm on any landscape, to learn
our gods have no bounds, sympathetic
most to those who do for themselves.

It could be foreign gibberish, a lost
native tongue, stirring coals, throwing
sticks upon the fire between us — that
rare communion of common souls
where almost Anyman can be a comedian.

for Tom, Sharon & Travis

GROWING OLD TOGETHER

There are two vast cottonwoods near a creek
when I walk between them I shiver.
           - Jim Harrison ("Doors")

Our buckeye portal, a perfect pair to pass through.
Killion and Snyder's yellow pines, side by side—
this partnership of trees for years near the top

of Sulphur, garnets, quartz and crystal, shafts
of granite thrust out of the earth as weathered
phallic totems among blue oak vast skies.

What words, what power lingers in the leaves,
whose dark eyes see more than mine, I wonder
with each welcome here—these gray limbs

dressed alike, or not at all, buckeyes arched
in season. Passing through either way
along this cow track refines the senses.

WAITING FOR DAYLIGHT

No alarm clock here, we take turns
waking-up on the hour before the first
branding of the year, lists of implements,

food and vaccines checked in our sleep
before heading up the hill, leaving
convenience for the make-do miles

off the asphalt where anything can happen
despite best-laid plans. We should be
too old, too accustomed to this drill

to toss and turn — we should be sure
and secure with familiar faces and horses,
good hands and neighbors come to help,

like always. Grown old together, we
understand what we have lost — yet shake
out another loop just to grin into the sun.

SWAMPERS

Headlights dancing down orchard rows,
silhouettes of men, half-loaded bob-tail
stuck in mud, getting oranges in
before the next rain and forecast freeze.

Unmuffled tractor groaning over shouts,
tight chain—there was no quittin' time
around Christmas in those days, no room
for church or grammar school recitals:

God helped those who helped themselves,
who made hay while the sun shined.
It's all we really knew of the world:
it took all year to raise a crop to sell.

Before non-cultivation, stinging nettles
high in a young boy's face, I followed men
swamping field boxes into the night,
and couldn't imagine a higher calling.

NOVEMBER SABBATH

The world is not what we thought it was.
- Jim Harrison ("Suite of Unreason")

Much done behind us, I listen in the dark
for predicted rain—like an old friend
I don't expect to arrive on time, if at all—

wondering if this day is mine to spend
without the human dramas spawned
on flat land for sudden hillsides, or will I

retreat, once again, to cows and calves,
to the chain saw's whine, go deeper under
the covers of this landscape to pray and

commiserate with my gods, those plural
and lower-cased forces at play that are
indeed the living wonders of this world:

groaking in the tops of gray oak trees,
scarlet hybrids, red-chested sapsuckers
none had seen this far south—bright

harbingers for a cold winter with the bumper
crop of acorns, black upon the ground—a
slim chance beyond that still makes sense.

A SIGN

Our moccasins do not mark the ground.
                - William Stafford ("Returned To Say")

We look for sign on soft ground,
something fresh from the past,
even the glint of a wing in the weeds

to draw us from the dusty track.
No one remembers their names,
all the old men or their sayings —

but they are here behind the page,
this side of tomorrow's sunrise.
They have set up camp, bedrolls

around a fire, each one helpless
as they survey landscapes shrink
and change a little everyday.

'He looks, but he just don't see,'
Tom Homer'd say of someone paid
to ride and look, set fences right

or watch the cattle slip away —
then lay down wagers with gentler
angels to pass his long reward.

Ground they know, riding ridges,
they can see what they want —
be entertained or disappointed

with humanity. We look for sign,
listen for whispers on native ground
from all the characters before us.

PERIPHERAL VISION

If you ever decide to quit
looking beyond the asphalt
buck-stitched by barb wire,

if you can't see either side
to your current destination
since you were a kid,

if your everyday is
planned and paced
to the drum of a clock,

you may not notice them
moving quickly to hide
just behind your ear.

DAYS

seemed so long, and weeks eternities
between recesses and vacations, lifetimes—
especially when ranch work replaced trouble.

Through the gate like cattle counted now,
they pass six or eight deep—heads, backs
and tails eclipsed and so blurred, we

might have missed one, or miscounted since
the beginning of time. There is a place, like
here, just after that, days had neither names

nor numbers, great herds grazing the planet,
eras when we might have lost a year or two
under endless skies guided by starlight.

GREASY 2010

It seems spring since November with
October rain and green, few frosty nights.
Just now, birds in the bare oaks practice

promising refrains, cows upcanyon quiet
with branded calves on damp, cool grass.
Not a hint of the buzz that marks the end

and we grin to one another, listen and grin
where generations have gathered, horses
tethered and irons grown cold, grinning

beneath Sulphur with a little spot of poppies
burning gold. Weathered smiles, we show
teeth and listen to our hearts howling.

- for Spencer Jensen

GUADALUPE 2

A slow song lingers on long days
under a 110 sun, Apollo reins to loiter
in the blue stretched between steep

horizons. Mind on the fuzzy edge
of delirium, lyric mantras arrive like
friends from 1965. I am thirsty,

just as naïve as then, listening
through poor acoustics to my
reshuffled rhymes reverberating,

new words to a familiar tune
inserted as the forgotten fade.
By noon, I can't look up to face

the light, blinded by harness silver
set afire, despite my *Atwood* palm
and diluted sun block leaking

down channels of emotion cut
deeper with time — the haunting
melody that begs to cry with,

and for, the persistent spirit
humbly camped within us
with a good lot on its mind.

for Tom Russell

WUKNAW

The metaphor of the forest is thick
with shadows, fleeting spirits lurking
in textured detail of hairy bark and moss

fuzzed on the edge of town, of commerce,
of self-indulgence — it's how we are. But
without the pocket gophers shaping boroughs

between rooted toes, or the screaming
scrub jays preening pine nut tresses,
we might not know how to survive.

Not far from here, Mountain Lion
sat down with all the animals to create
humans. No one can remember why.

CHRISTMAS 2010

The dead,
too, denying their graves, haunt
the places they were known in and knew,
field and barn, riverbank and woods.
- Wendell Berry ("2008, X.")

Even now the headstones claim
little flats beneath nameless draws
either side of the house, rough

granite boulders set at the head
of deep holes filled for horse and dog—
where the deer lay down to shade

when I was a boy, and women healed
the spirit, burning sage, chanting
until they fell asleep. Hollow ground

to horses' hooves where my children
played pretend, those great imaginings
that beg to fly—now walk their sons,

listening—feet wet in grass.
To come home for Christmas can be
a gift—so many voices welcoming.

LETTER TO LINDA HASSELSTROM

Dear Linda, I think of you driving nights
between snow banks, long distances
between farm house lights and little
towns flickering ahead—I think of resolve
to turn a word to fit the truth, hard facts
that wear the heart smooth and bodies out.
I think of you peering under the corral boards,
the love and fear of it, graphic words
jumping off your tongue on their own.
We could make a movie together, gray
reflections in the middle of nowhere,
turning the barnyard upside down
for another look at the world, another
look at why we're here, at why a life
without some small purpose beyond ourselves—
a waste of time and flesh—better fertilizer
on the prairie to be blown to another place.
Meet you in Elko to read some poetry—
separated by soothing melodies, the cloak
of the old songs, guitars and accordion,
to keep us warm. Looking forward, John.

EARTH SONG

Slow steps across distance growing
shorter, oak shade with springs leaking
out of the ground, cracks in the granite

savored now with the first breath drawn
by men, men and women, children after
children becoming part of the same

moment, a millisecond or so, back.
Their songs still linger here, echo
in the canyons, grow to the dark side

of rocks like velvet moss refreshed
by rain or grin defiantly with lichen—
sparks of fire towards the sun.

I don't need to understand the words—
the song is enough—an old melody
holding ground just off the road.

YOU MAY NOT KNOW THEM

Chance and fate, we fly through time
on pinball ricochets and peg collisions
with bells and whistles, defying gravity

until our turn is done. Few measure each
extended breath or look to granite peaks
with awe, but early-on someone calls —

a distant whisper or the wild songs
that resonate beyond our knowing —
and they choose, drawn like water

to its groove, the gravity of grounded
things that grow, that root, that leaf
that fruit, that bear and live to bear

again like grass with rain. Your hands
may not show calloused content, nor
eyes absorb a lifelong harvest, but

they are scattered here and there
like grazing cattle, simple people who
feed themselves — who feed us all.

DREAMS & VISIONS

Always her ankle at the head of Live Oak Canyon,
toes reaching Sulphur Peak, long legs stretching south
to Rabbit Flat, to her breasts freckled with Blue Oaks

when the full moon hangs like a pendant beneath them
glowing as she sleeps, rising as she breathes, dark
hair cascading between canyons spilling into the creek.

The women who gathered here, gossiped and ground
what they found, spent nights away from men to heal
themselves—they must have seen her first from here,

alive and breathing, heaving with these hills of flesh—
solstice to solstice, sun kissing the length of her body
trying to awaken the dreams and visions in our sleep.

BRILLIANT DARKNESS

…as in the night when there is no moon
I must have known it once
    - Robert Mezey ("I Am Beginning to Hear")

Or rusty bucket leaking starlight upside down,
pinholes to the lasting sun near heaven once
high in the granite where chilly air turns crystalline—

we were but boys, young mountain men
around a fire. But even then, I must have known
beneath that thin thimble of the old ones, must have

overheard their voices when I faced blue tongues
upon the coals. Tamarack, bold tamarack, ever
listening from the rock beneath the snows.

One is playing upon the lute, another braiding
rivers into a knot, making small talk in our dreams
and then remembers to lift the lid near dawn again—

bell mare restless in the cold. I must have known it
then, and now confined by time awake in black space,
the familiar voices, sweet idle chatter leaking in.

ONE NEVER KNOWS

It could as well be acorns arranged,
sorted and stored for winter—brittle
manzanita in the corner, anxious oak

under eve. We could as well be gophers
or woodpeckers anticipating cold or wet,
or both in this canyon that supported

three hundred humans, I'm told. In the air,
even the forgotten are making preparations,
busy leaping beams of horizontal light

burning at its edges like a grass fire.
Fall has come dressed like spring, teasing
suspiciously, vibrantly upon the green—

it is tempting to let old eyes go, follow her
off into the shadow of something new,
dark and grand that surely looms ahead.

Or it could be time has slowed the limbs
to seek simplicity, search each step—a
time to look beyond the maze of memory

and breathe, accept—ready the senses
to let instincts play with fresh words, the
honest and untrained upon our tongues.

HOPE IS IN THE MOMENT

We are cast of stone, all kinds,
no two the same, amalgamations
worn by time's erosion, by

wind, sun and rain — warming,
soothing, eating away towards
the core of our ultimate humility.

Even the lofty falcon's perch,
gray-haired, exfoliates into the sea,
the Sierra's teeth crumbling and

the cobble found to fit a hand
are finally sand, gravel for highways,
particles of dust stirred and inhaled

as strangers remembered, carried
in our chests. What do the eyes
truly see, searching for that mystic

connection of great and small, those
depths we explore where details meet
and fall in love, or lust, or like —

or as we gird for battle? Here,
in that moment there is no time
to relive the past or dream of some

future futility. The real action churns
with it all at once, in the current
like a river rushing, pooling, soaking

richly within us, before moving on.

VISITING THE FUTURE

Early afternoon on the
way up the mountain,
the past phones ahead — says
she is *Margaret, my* dead
mother. Are we
too busy for a visit?

We can start anywhere,
hollering hellos and goddamn
profanities as pickup doors
fly open to handshakes and
hugs. *How long has it been?*

Mule packers, horse lovers
wearing outdoor eyes —
who've caught God
drooling at his easel
on every horizon, every
turn of King's Canyon,
Rio de los Santos Reyes,

guffaw at our little bit
of Crown and Jack, *got
one in the truck,* want
nothing, but help speed
the recycling of glass
— unscrew new jugs
to a list of things to do
before dark, up the hill
and narrow road, nearly
empty weekdays without
the caravans of Christians
and 4-wheel drive crazies
racing towards heaven.

We catch up with highlights
of kids and grandkids,
weddings and fencing jobs,
pick fruit, swap books
and make promises to
rivers of fish, to the future
trails we will cross.

- for Tim & Maggie

A SOLITARY GAME

Some things need to be saved, but not poetry's
shuffle of words to fit an illusive moment
like shackles and chains bound in a book,

not the euphoric epiphanies we stumbled onto
out on the trail alone, or running the dark roads
between settlements of distant light, not those

rambling soliloquies when the radio fades
to poor company. It's a solitary game
on the other side of numbers, pat answers

and scientific proof—primal sounds to mark
a trek beyond the veil of certainty shuffled
with the landscape and its latest inhabitants.

Elegies

not to savor grief, but to collect
what parts we can, to piece our nest
back-together again.
                -JCD ("If We Have Love")

DECEMBER THIRD

She doesn't know what day it is,
that it would have been his
ninety-first — I say, 'Thursday.'

Forehead in hand, elbow on the arm
of her wheelchair, bonnet binding
white hair untrained, we argue

about a doctor, going out in public
without prosthesis beneath the pastel
tent sagging from her shoulders.

She is surprised that it's not important,
that no one's left alive in Visalia
she might know — that I don't care.

Words like badminton, she hides her face,
as concepts tumble loosely beneath
alabaster fingers pressed into resolve

and I see her father, hear her tone
in the last refrain of all the songs
of pioneers — 'I'm trying, John.'

COWTOWN 2009

A little girl, her father sent her
inside, when he washed the blood
of brandings from his hands—
oak and hair, the pungent mix
of smoke still swirling round him.

She spends more time looking
down now at her own
translucent skin, deep blue rivers
running through her alabaster flesh
folded in her wheelchair.

She says it doesn't feel
like Visalia anymore, born
and raised, endured eighty-five
years in the same place
she never noticed changing.

How she hated duty and
obligation—World War Two
and the love that flew away,
never to come back through
the door of her perfect cage.

Not the fairytale ending,
she closes the book and waits
for a menu, understands
that no one's left
to protect her from this.

DELICATE

cymbidiums exchanged for each occasion
between old girlfriends reduced by time—
lavish gestures of one-upmanship, but

she wants something SPECIAL,
bigger, better, custom arranged and tall
by Valentine's, for Bill and Jane

on their anniversary, for all
the belated birthdays she's forgotten,
ordered a month in advance in case she dies.

Bill downstairs, arms black and heavy,
motionless—tubes and machines.
Jane hobbles without a cane between

floors, not escaping what is etched
in the elevator, on hospital walls
and the faces that neither acknowledge—

all waiting for their world to get better.
I have lied—waiting too,
for the order of things.

4 SOUTH 24

In the shadow of the fallen
limb, waist-sized carcass
the grass is swallowing —

on the dark side there,
something beautiful, ex-
citing, you've never seen

quite. We part green stems
like curtains and there,
a child again playing games

by herself — preferring
clear the hell away
from her mother's shrill

pomposity fixed
on what she is not.
And her mother, the

teetotaler that married
the old judge who hid
in the barn with his jug.

Even now, I can hear it
pierce rooms through
the big house, the faux-

operatic screeched keyless
to hello yodels at the door
in those days — so senseless

now, but she's OK
playing princess
for as long as she can.

THAT'S HOW IT GOES

> *I used to remember everything that happened*
> *plain as the love on her face. Now it mixes*
> *and fades.*
> > - Richard Hugo ("How Meadows
> > Trick You")

Sweet indulgences on the unimproved ground,
the picturesque, the rough and tough, entwined with
    similes,
lasting metaphors invested in the same place

that has changed a little on it's own along the creek.
Was it my birthday in '68 or '69, twenty or twenty-one in
    love
with someone, or not — wet feet beneath the sycamores

walking after a wet spring, huge high-channel puddles
reflecting blue and cumulus through naked limbs – I may
    have
even cried, and they may have held me there

forever here, until the miners felled them. Canada
was the question, as I stole photographs to take back to
    school
to share, to hold before I gave that future up.

That's how it goes along braided creeks, memories
that can be shaped and improved by lots of rain, rafts of
    deadfall
redirecting flows, carving faces in their cobbled banks.

LAST NIGHT'S LEFTOVERS

We pray for heart attacks, Mack trucks and lightening
as our way out, trading tales of die-hard mothers
like rattlesnake stories, each triggering another—

pouring wine with whiskey rants to laugh
at the sad truth we can't improve, can't make easier,
can't change, but in ourselves. Out of the rain,

my great bay horse, a bag of bones at thirty,
paws the gate in the barn for more grain—an indignant
impatience I trained for years, my mother's hands

in mine again. It's rained five days straight,
blew the barn down, blew a tire in a rockslide,
got a ticket parked too long at the hospital,

and we look up into the gray wanting to escape
town and traffic, find home and recuperate
with neighbors and last night's leftovers.

                                    - for Steve & Jody

WEDNESDAY

My horse is not sure he can make it
to the next star. You are free.
- Richard Hugo ("To Women")

The burden the stork brought, *you start it all* —
a child then filled with dreams, you bore
your fears and learned with me. Black soot,

roadways inflamed with smudge pot sentries,
red helmets straight for miles into the night,
always crystalline, dark rafts above by day,

for weeks. Checking temperatures,
starting wind machines, climbing towers
towards the props on flat-head Ford V8s

roaring in his ears, he was a bear asleep
before the fire, diesel sweater, when we
awoke into the smells of his dark nights.

Dialysis, thoracentesis you refuse and send
them packing, only to ask next morning,
if you heard the Doctor right — 'another day?'

'Day by day,' I think he said —
all of us learning together once more
how to die, how to live each breath, at last.

WOLF MOON 2010

Already pictures in from London, Chip beneath
a lighter stack of books tonight, his burden
of literature lifting a little, shifting towards

his homeland and shaky California, but we
have yet to feel the darkness. Yet to see the wolf
clear the sharp Sierras between here and Elko.

We are all apart, each undone by distance, yet
together in tonight's sky. I trust my mother
anticipates the proper moonbeam as she

trains her wings. Driving home at dawn,
the sun leaked like spotlights upon the Yokohl,
angling through low gray openings, snow

upon the Kaweah peaking into the light rain—
the kind of glory artists have captured in oil
for centuries. One must thank someone

for the real thing. She is not religious, despite
her hands folded across her breastless chest,
shoulders quivering in unison as she sleeps.

We imagine angels adjusting and attaching
feathers, a fluttering with the rising moon
we share with her ascension from this flesh.

PEACE OFFERING

An eagle floating, feathers glint like
burnished brass above upcanyon green,
perhaps the same who claimed the breech,

coyote at bay and she, a black and helpless
silhouette under the tree where she labored —
a pitiful strain of motherhood to be admired.

I follow my eyes like the shadow I was
behind my father, tried to match his stride,
always listening, then asking for more.

A few old men still remember the boy,
breaking clods behind the tractor with little
boots, or behind the four and five year-olds

from Mexico, right off the train
across the bridge and up the road until
belly-high in heaven. But they're not

my eyes anymore, I cannot own
the current that flows between us —
the peace that connects all things.

LAND OF NO SECRETS

Has he grown weary waiting, found another,
or wandered-off into the wilderness of heaven,
beyond the waves of the cerebral telegraph

that you are arriving soon? So long ago—
the war that pulled him down, it hurts
to anticipate, to contemplate his warmth,

his touch – gone before I came along
to fill his spot as your first born. Are you
giddy and afraid to leave to take so long

to say good-bye, to shed this craziness
that all the angels crave, staying busy—
or will you have to go to work to heal

the wounds from your barbed tongue,
once you let yourself be loved again?
Don't you know? There are no secrets now.

OUR CENOTAPH

Today I remember the pieces, deep
reds and blues of my mother's Imari
glued to Mary Hadley's farm scenes—

a fractured clash of bright and pale
that fit somehow to make a landscape
I can abide, but better on the borders

of the garden. With each glazed shard,
we till and plant our grief, a glint of color
for tomorrow's tomatoes and squash.

I want to plant something in her
grand twenty-gallon vase that's only
held umbrellas on its carved oak stand

half-century in a dark and dusty corner.
I want to bring it back to life, make it
useful in a pagan coup d'état that sings

with art fading in the weather, as we
all do in time, a song that celebrates
owning nothing with this flesh.

A place she can visit for coffee
and a cigarette, make suggestions
while we work the earth.

AS SHE SLEEPS

Ranges of foothills fall sharply from clouds
stacked against Sierra snow, pastel ridges
washed pink and lavender under light gray rain —

I want to stop and paint them from the railroad
overpass, on the highway from Visalia — park
and stop time, freeze it all while I brush

powder to paper. Commuting now for weeks,
I can read the leanings of the urgent
escaping work, racing towards something

somewhere I can't imagine as important
as these mountains — a different meaning
in the light of every day. Wrinkled one

behind the other, I identify each dark line
as it jags into the Kaweah like the folds
of bedclothes as she sleeps, going home.

GIRLFRIENDS

It happens, little rafts of deadfall rise,
ease downstream and build into a flood
of memories that fill the mind, that seep

and irrigate the forgotten ground — little
boy, pastoral scenes for the innocent.
I can see you both over the phone, Cut's

rodear at Badger — your father, the butcher —
as little girls, one leading, one riding
the old mule, shouting over the rattlesnake

you uncovered. Beef on the fire with beans
and booze, Cut loved the spectacle of wild
times shared a short drive from town friends

that first night out. When all the old hands
I knew were cowboys then, willow shoots
collecting dew just up the canyon.

It happens, little rafts of deadfall rise, all
broken loose in stories from dear friends
that spill and wash, leave us clean again.

for Jane, Lorie, Marilyn, Helen & Peggy

UNEVEN GREEN

Little do we know of that ground
between the lush, iridescent hills
and that beyond them, except

it's magical. How some days
it rains with coincidence when
we're most vulnerable and open,

so helpless within ourselves —
powerless to ignore the obvious.
You can feel the shuffling

of spirits, of ghosts, or angels slip
upcanyon to make the forgotten
connections to the old world —

set up camp and start a fire. The air
sings songs, one after another until
all harmonize to make you feel

like leaving your flesh, almost
blindly reaching out to touch,
and hold, what you know

very little about — like young calves
just running and bucking across
uneven green because they can.

PHALAENOPSIS

Tall shadow on the morning wall,
like a person waiting in the dark
when I awake without a mother,

now planted atop my father
like shoeboxes in a black closet
I'll never open — only to drive by

       with a nod to the gods
       in case they're listening.

Cast from the desk lamp,
she comes alive when I rise
to get more coffee, changes

shape and grins with gestures.
The one she gave Robbin
has bloomed every year

since her father died, white
faces reaching for the light
when we'd return from Elko —

after ten cold days in a stale
empty house, looking out at Sulphur
as our sweet 'welcome home'.

INVITATION

We have rain and plenty work, stacking-up
across the creek, the garden always calling
for a visit. Nothing's changed all that much.

Not like the days and nightmares, he left behind
when he took-off for parts unknown.
You made it easy, kept everyone away

with insistent wishes your friends ignored.
This year's calves from your black cows
may be the best ones yet, with all this grass.

Take a look, first chance you get—I know
we say it every year, but they'll weigh-up
like little bears. And the wildflowers, Mom…

it's worth a visit around the equinox. The kids
are driving, flying-in to gather in the garden—
plant something special for you to find!

John Dofflemyer's family began raising cattle in the Sierra Nevada foothills of Tulare County in 1852, where he and his wife Robbin are engaged in a cow and calf operation on Dry Creek, a tributary of the Kaweah River. The founding editor and publisher of the *Dry Crik Review*, author of thirteen collections of poetry and included in several anthologies, his 'Poems from Dry Creek', published by Starhaven, received the Wrangler Award from the National Cowboy and Western Heritage Museum in April, 2009. He and Robbin have maintained the weblog, *Dry Crik Journal – Perspectives from the Ranch* with photographs and poetry since 2005.

http://drycrikjournal.wordpress.com

~

Other titles by John Dofflemyer:

Dry Creek Rhymes
Sensin' Somethin'
Muses of the Ranges
Black Mercedes
Cattail and other poems
Hung Out to Dry
Shrewd Angles and other poems
Still in the Mountains
April Bullfrogs
Poems from Dry Creek
2009 – Dry Crik Journal
Elegies
Uneven Green

www.ingramcontent.com/pod-product-compliance
Lightning Source LLC
Chambersburg PA
CBHW020911090426

42736CB00008B/573